THOMAS & FRIENDS™

MEET THE ENGINES

Written by Julia March

CONTENTS

WELCOME TO SODOR

Harwick

Whiff's Recycling Plant

Duck Pond

Tidmouth

McColl's Farm

Maintenance Yard

Wellsworth

Suddery

Brendam Docks

N
W E
S

Thomas knows **Sodor** like the back of his buffers. That's because **railway tracks** go all over the **island**—to stations, docks, mountains, woods, castles, and mines. Is there a **corner** of Sodor that Thomas has not yet visited? **He doesn't think so!**

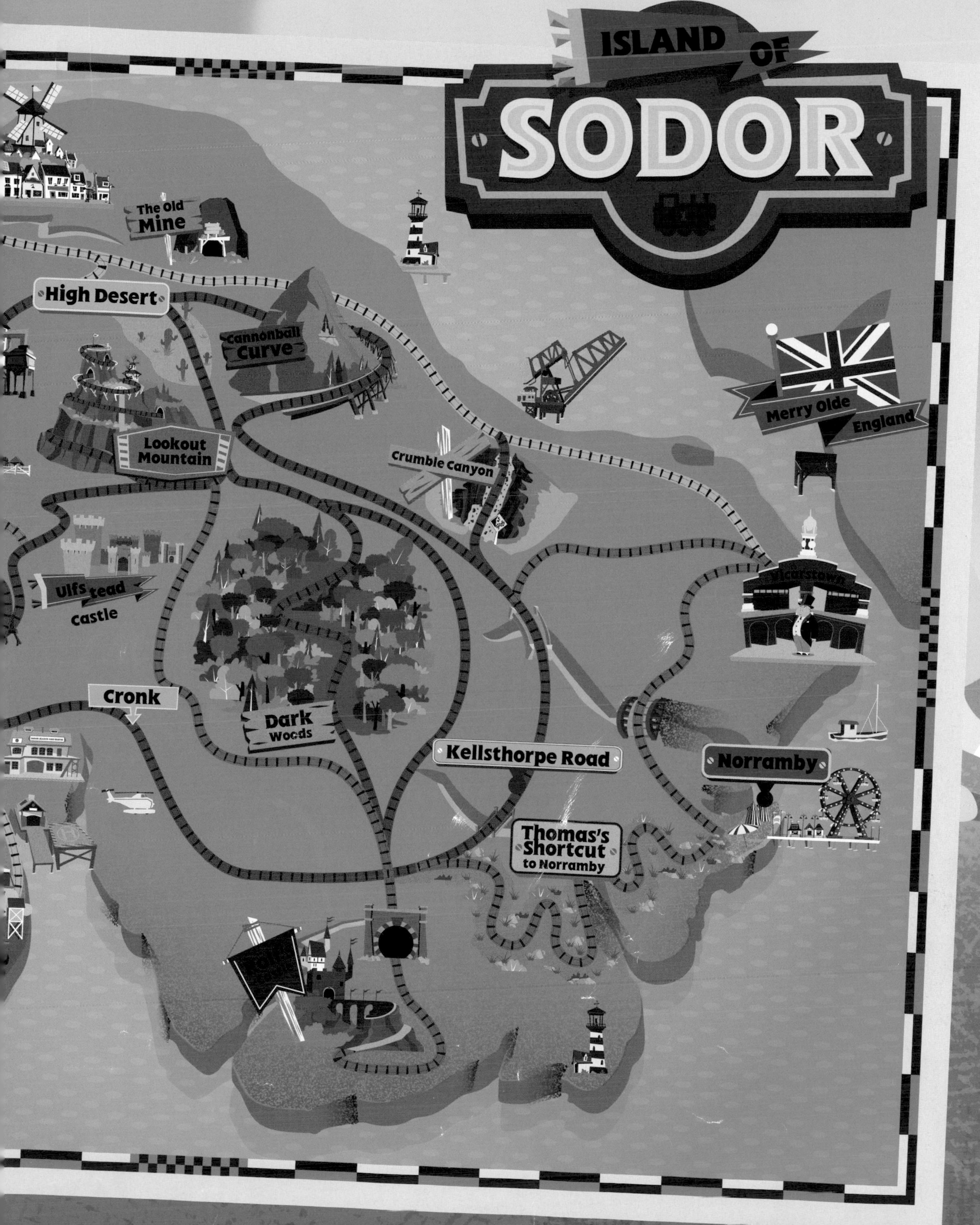

ISLAND OF

SODOR

The Old Mine

High Desert

Cannonball Curve

Lookout Mountain

Crumble Canyon

Merry Olde England

Vicarstown

Ulfstead Castle

Cronk

Dark Woods

Kellsthorpe Road

Norramby

Thomas's Shortcut to Norramby

MEET THE TEAM

Thomas's closest **friends** are the four engines who share his home at **Tidmouth Sheds**. They are Kana, Nia, Percy, and Diesel. Thomas thinks they are "**toot-ally awesome!**"

"All engines go!"

THOMAS
The tank engine

This cheeky little engine always tries to do his best. He may be small, but he is very brave. That is why Thomas has lots of friends!

Stacks of fun

Thomas loves to stack his cargo high—with a little help from Carly! Teamwork gets the job done!

Did you know?

Thomas is based on an old E2-class steam engine from 100 years ago.

 **FACT FILE**

Home: Tidmouth Sheds

Works with: His faithful coaches Annie and Clarabel

Likes: Making friends

FUN FACT!
Thomas's whistle makes a "peep peep" sound.

Thomas greets his friends with a smile

Number 1 is painted on his side tank

He has six wheels

One day, Thomas got **paint** splattered over the 1 on his side. Did it mean he was no longer the **Number 1 Engine**? He began to think so when he had a bad day and arrived **late** and **dirty** with his delivery. But **Sir Topham Hatt** said Thomas would always be Number 1.

> **"You're Number 1 because I can count on you!"**
> **said Sir Topham Hatt**

PERCY

Thomas's best friend

Little Percy loves fun as much as Thomas, but he is not so adventurous. He is happy to let his friend take the lead. And that's just fine!

On the mo-o-o-ve

"Old McColl had a farm ..." Percy and Thomas sing to make delivering cows even more fun.

 **FACT FILE**

Works with: Thomas

Likes: Delivering mail

Dislikes: Roller coasters, the dark, and pandas

Careful Percy

Percy likes everything to run smoothly. Before making a delivery, he carefully checks the route.

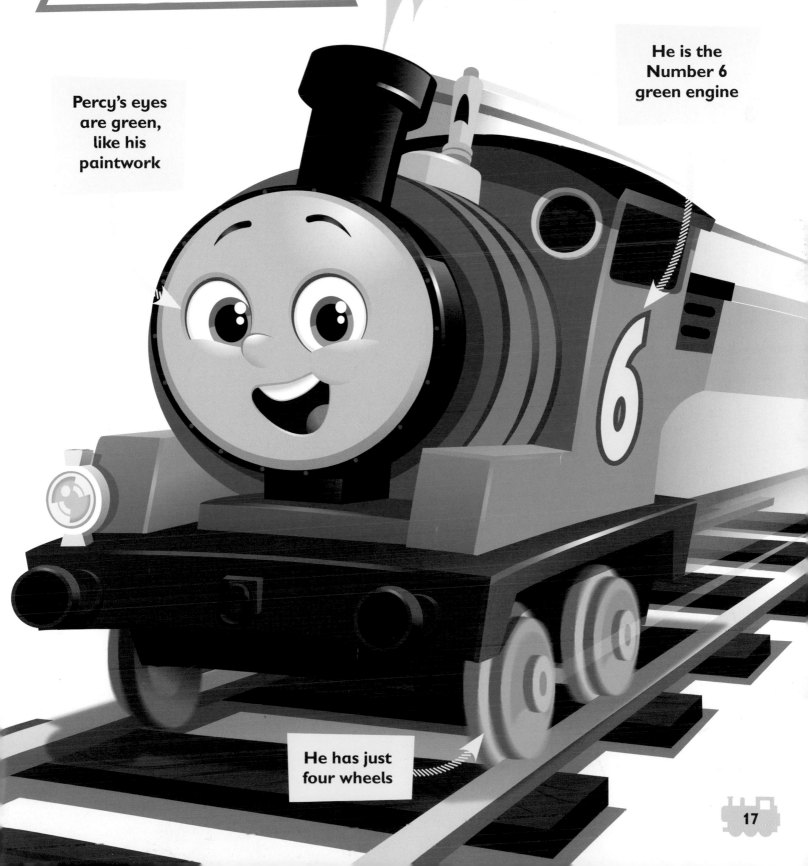

"That's what I call Percy perfect!"

FUN FACT!
Percy has a lucky bell that he rings when he feels a bit scared.

He is the Number 6 green engine

Percy's eyes are green, like his paintwork

He has just four wheels

Percy thought **roller coasters** were scary. Just seeing one at a carnival made his gears **shake**. But after **Thomas**, **Nia**, and **Kana** helped him face his fears, Percy felt ready to try out a **loop the loop**. He ended up going **around, and around, and around** ...

"They're so fast, and so screamy, and so upside-down!"
said Percy

NIA

The engine full of ideas

This fun-loving engine comes from Kenya, in Africa. She's kind and caring, and loves thinking up new, creative ways to do things. Everyone loves Nia!

A cheerful song

At an overnight stop, Percy is scared to sleep outdoors. Kind Nia cheers him up with a campfire song.

A bridge too far

Not all Nia's ideas work out. Trying to dash over a faulty drawbridge is a big mistake.

FACT FILE

Comes from: Kenya

Role: Pulling cargo or passengers

Likes: Traveling and seeing new places

66 Wow! I made a new sound! 99

Nia usually wears a big, bright smile

FUN FACT!
Nia has invented a dance called the "Piston Pop."

Kenyan pattern on tank

She has eight orange wheels

21

"Hmm ... the balloon is bigger than I planned!"
said Nia

Nia was carrying a **train-shaped balloon** to Vicarstown for a parade. She decided to take **Floaty** through a **tunnel**, where the wind couldn't blow it away. But, oh dear—what a **tight squeeze**! With a big push from **Kana** and **Thomas**, they just about got through.

KNAPFORD STATION

Situated to the west, Knapford Station is the **largest** station in Sodor. Working engines come and go all day at this **busy** station. Its graceful **glass roofs** and **spacious platforms** make it a perfect place for **special events**, too!

SIR TOPHAM HATT

The railway owner

Sir Topham owns the railway. He also arranges all the special events in Sodor. This jolly gentleman is rarely seen without his hat, except when the wind blows it away!

Musical mix-up

When instruments for a concert go missing, Sir Topham is eager to track them down. "The show must go on!" he says.

> **66 See you all at the parade! 99**

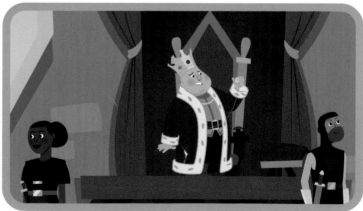

King Topham

Sir Topham enters into the spirit of all his events. For a medieval faire, he dresses in full king's regalia.

FUN FACT!
Close friends call Sir Topham by his first name—Bertram.

JAMES
The really splendid engine

Is James the most handsome engine in Sodor? He certainly thinks so! But when he stops fussing about his paintwork, James is a lot of fun.

James's brass parts are well polished

He wears a dazzling coat of scarlet paint

FACT FILE

Type: Tender engine

Likes: Being admired

Dislikes: Getting his paint dirty, or even worse—scratched!

Dragon!
James panics when he comes face to face with a model dragon made for a medieval faire. He thinks it's a real one!

66 Mind my paintwork! 99

Junction jostle
When a signal failure causes a snarl-up at a junction, arrogant James tries to push through before Diesel. Bump!

Perfectly buffed buffers

FUN FACT!
James thinks he would make an "unbearably charming" knight.

29

HENRY
The Number 3 green engine

Henry is a big green engine who chugs around wishing everyone a breezy "Good morning!" He is a bit of a worrier and prefers calm days.

Barrier bother

During a power outage, Henry got stuck at a signal. He didn't have to worry for long. Carly arrived and raised the barrier for him.

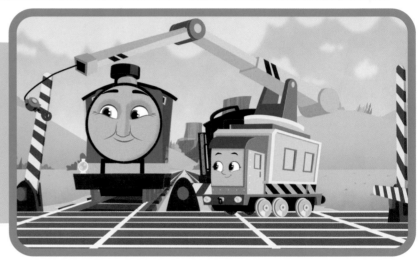

His steam dome is gold

Henry's face reflects his mood

🚂 FACT FILE

Home: Vicarstown

Favorite job: Pulling cargo trains

Likes: Good manners and respect

EDWARD

The old, reliable engine

Good old Edward! He's patient, wise, kind, and very hardworking. With years of experience under his buffers, Edward is ready for anything!

Stop, Edward!
Quickdraw Bridge began to lift just as Edward was about to puff onto it. He made a quick stop!

FACT FILE

Age: Who knows?

Likes: Stories set in the past

Dislikes: Being teased about his age

His linings are red

Gentle, cheerful smile

❝ I'm ready! ❞

DIESEL
Thomas's friendly rival

This pushy little diesel engine never stops challenging Thomas to games and races. Oh, how he would love to beat his friend ... just once!

Diesel puffs out thick gray smoke

He speeds along on six wheels

Coupling hook lets him link with other vehicles

Did you know?

Diesel is based on a British Rail Class 08 shunter from the 1950s. Some Class 08s are still in service today.

🚂 FACT FILE

Home: Tidmouth Sheds

Works with: Thomas and his friends

Dream: To be Sodor's "real Number 1 Engine"

Dirty tricks

In a race to Whiff's Recycling Plant, Diesel tries to slow Thomas down by puffing smoke in his face. That's not fair!

66 See you at the finish line! 99

FUN FACT!
Diesel got starstruck when he met two famous race engines.

"Well, we are the Bigger Adventure Club!" said Diesel

Thomas, Percy, and Carly formed an adventure club to look for a **Crystal Cave** in the Old Mine. **Diesel** and **Sandy** formed a **rival** club, hoping to get there first. It was a great **team-up**! Sandy squeezed easily through tiny spaces, and Diesel did the **heavy lifting**.

MAINTENANCE YARD

The Maintenance Yard is where **Sandy and Carly** work, fixing **broken-down engines** with a smile. The **workshops** look a bit **jumbled**, but the duo always find just the tool they need.

CARLY

The little crane on wheels

If anything needs lifting or shifting, the engines call on Carly. This chirpy little crane will whizz to the scene. Carly's partner, Sandy, is her best friend.

Museum mix-up

Assembling a dinosaur skeleton is tricky. Carly keeps getting the bones in the wrong order.

 **FACT FILE**

Home: Maintenance Yard

Role: Lifting, loading, and helping fix things

Works with: Sandy

Patient Carly

Carly helps Thomas build an obstacle course, but it takes up all her patience. Thomas is very picky indeed!

There are hazard stripes on her boom

Carly's hook is attached to a strong cable

66Let's get lifting!99

Laying tracks is part of Carly's job

39

SANDY
Everyone's fix-it friend

Sandy can fix anything, from a hole in a tank to a wobbly wheel. This tiny speeder has a toolbox full of scoops, wrenches, saws, and hammers.

Yellow emergency light

Sandy's job can get her a bit dirty

Toolbox at the front

Stop, Thomas!
Sandy must stop Thomas quickly—some ducks are on the line. Luckily, she has a stop sign on board.

🚂 FACT FILE

Home: Maintenance Yard

Works with: Carly

Likes: Making sand sculptures

Too little?
Thomas said Sandy was too little to join his "Big Adventure Club." What a nerve!

❝ Make way for the Sandy express! ❞

⭐ FUN FACT!
Playing in mud is Sandy's idea of fun. After all, mud is wet sand!

One day, a **rainbow** appeared over Sodor. The **engines** wanted to find the end of the rainbow. But it was at the top of a tall, twisty **mountain**, and the track was broken. **Carly** and **Sandy** worked to **repair** the track so they could go up, up, and over to the rainbow's end.

"With a crack crack here and a snap snap there ..."
sang Carly and Sandy

GORDON

The engine in charge

Gordon is a wise engine who supervises the other engines. He is kind but stern and wants everything done his way. The right way!

Do as you're told!
Thomas and Percy get a real telling-off when they disobey Gordon's instructions.

 **FACT FILE**

Home: Knapford Station

Works with: All the engines, and also Sir Topham Hatt

Likes: Giving orders

Mystery gift
Gordon has a sense of humor. He leaves some machinery for Kana in a gift-wrapped box car for her to find.

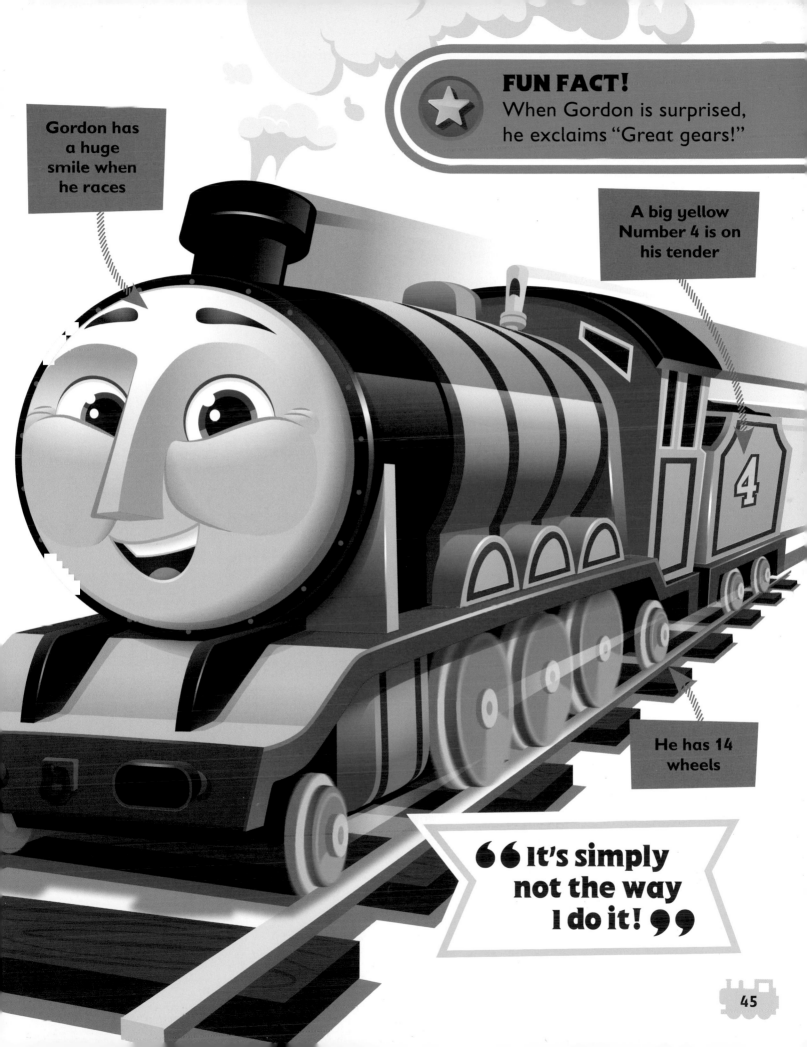

Gordon has a huge smile when he races

A big yellow Number 4 is on his tender

He has 14 wheels

66 It's simply not the way I do it! 99

Gordon usually knows what to do in an emergency. But when the **switch** that lowers **Quickdraw Bridge** got stuck, Gordon was stuck, too. How would he get across the river? **Thomas** and his friends had to help Carly **pull** the bridge down and **rescue** Gordon.

66 The switch that lowers the bridge is stuck! 99
said Gordon

EMILY
The safety engine

Emily is proud to be Sodor's official safety engine. She's prevented many a disaster, from train accidents to Sir Topham Hatt's hat blowing away.

Flying flag

When Thomas lost control of a parade flag, even Emily couldn't stop it from landing on Sir Topham Hatt!

Confident smile

🚂 FACT FILE

Role: Saving the day

Works with: All the engines

Likes: Restoring calm after chaos

Red buffer beam

ASHIMA
The mountain engine

Heights hold no fear for Ashima—she works on a mountain railway in India. When Ashima visited Sodor, her fancy paintwork caught everyone's eye.

 FACT FILE

Comes from: India

Best friend: Thomas—she encourages him to challenge himself

Likes: Shunting

⭐ **FUN FACT!**
Ashima's name means "without limits" in the Hindi language.

Hot pink is her main color

Ashima has a calm, gentle expression

She has brightly colored decals all over her

❝ **Be who you are and go far!** ❞

49

KENJI
The silver racer

Sleek, silver Kenji is a high-speed electric train who wins races all over the world. Kenji is super smart and super fast, but super modest, too.

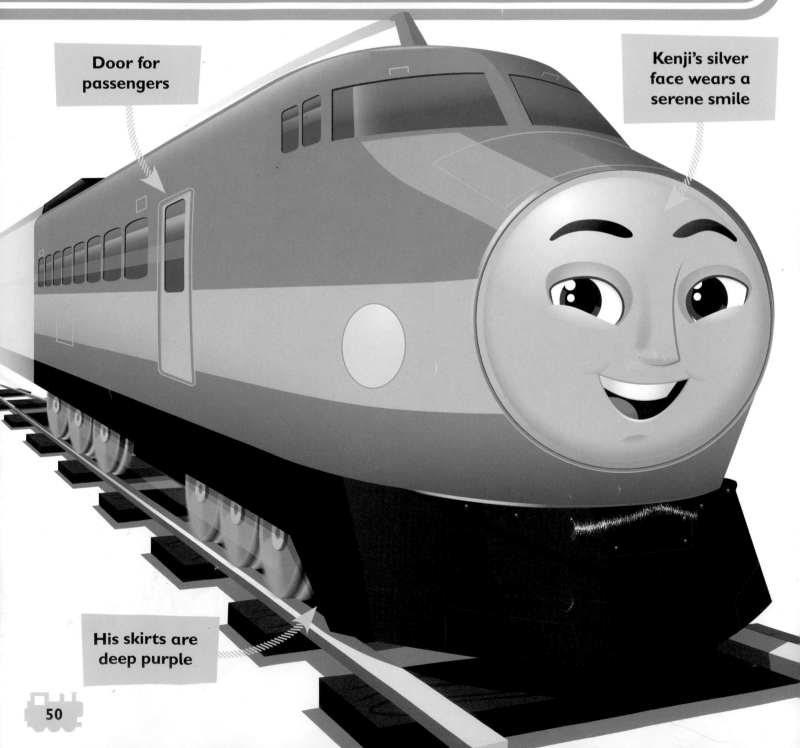

Door for passengers

Kenji's silver face wears a serene smile

His skirts are deep purple

FACT FILE

Comes from: Japan

Works with: Kana, mostly. She can usually keep up with him!

Ambition: To win the Sodor Cup with Kana

Did you know?

Kenji is based on a 0 series Shinkansen engine—a super-fast "bullet train" from Japan.

Going bust

When Kana nearly crashes, Kenji busts a fender trying to stop her. Is he out of the race for the Sodor Cup?

66 **Don't let them get to you.** 99

FUN FACT!

Kenji is very ticklish. He giggles as Sandy examines his fender.

ANNIE AND CLARABEL

Kindly coaches

These two comfy coaches travel together, usually pulled by Thomas. They love pretty scenery and like to snooze on night trips.

Pretty risky

Crumble Canyon is very pretty, but also very dangerous. Look out for falling rocks!

FACT FILE

Role: Giving passengers tours of Sodor

Best friend: Each other

Likes: Thomas—except when he makes a noise and wakes them up!

Sleep tight

Annie and Clarabel are settling down to sleep. Carly kindly puts a snuggly blanket over them.

FUN FACT!
Until recently, Clarabel preferred to travel facing backward.

The patterns on their sides are different

Kind, caring expression

They like a steady pace

Only Clarabel has freckles

❝We're taking the scenic route!❞

BRENDAM DOCKS

Brendam Docks is a **large port** that handles all **goods** coming to or from Sodor. It is home to **Cranky**, who spends his days grumpily hoisting **cargo** between Bulstrode and the waiting engines.

54

CRANKY
The grumpy crane

This big crane works at Brendam Docks. Cranky gets grumpy when engines mess around. But he always sees the funny side in the end.

> **Hey ... enough playing around!**

⭐ **FUN FACT!**
Cranky got Percy used to heights by whirling him around!

Helpful Cranky
Cranky is helpful when engines are polite. He is happy to give Thomas a lift onto Bulstrode.

That's funny!
When a truck full of confetti explodes all over Diesel, Cranky just has to laugh. Ha, ha, ha!

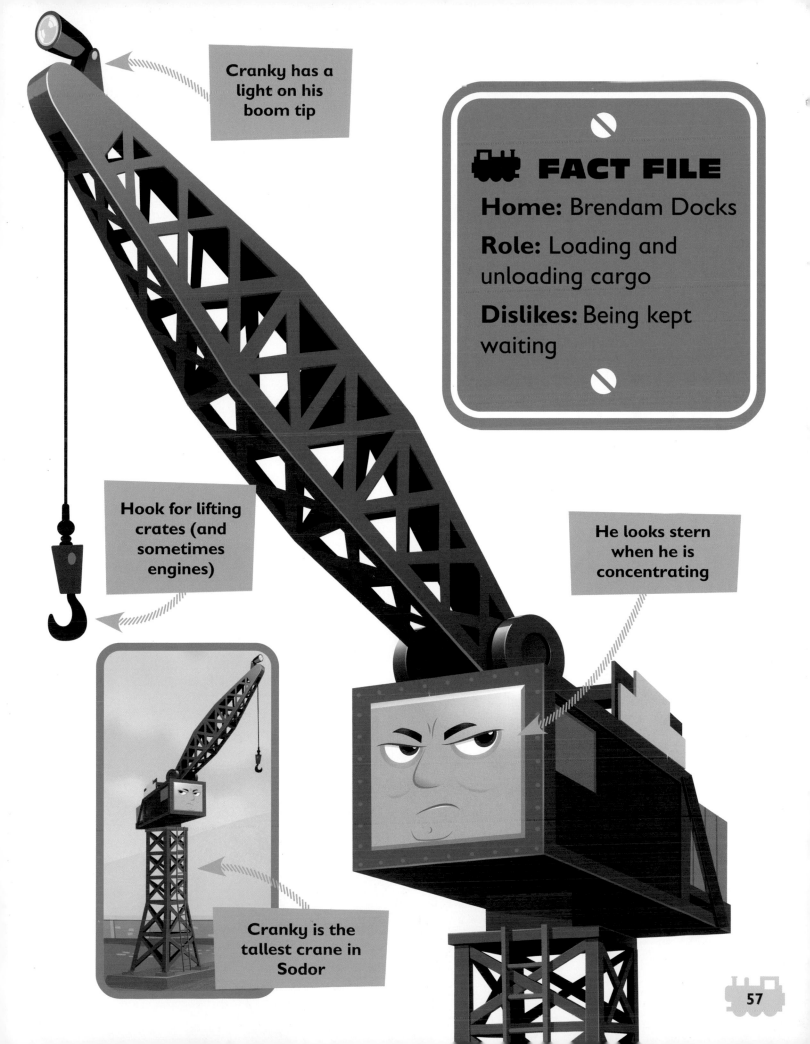

Cranky has a light on his boom tip

FACT FILE

Home: Brendam Docks

Role: Loading and unloading cargo

Dislikes: Being kept waiting

Hook for lifting crates (and sometimes engines)

He looks stern when he is concentrating

Cranky is the tallest crane in Sodor

There was to be a **rocket launch** at **Brendam Docks**. Each engine brought one of the rocket parts. **Thomas** was supposed to bring the **battery**. But he thought it was **too small** to be very important, so he forgot! **Cranky** wasn't very happy about that!

"Thomas, the rocket can't take off without your battery!" grumbled Cranky

BULSTRODE

The laidback barge

Bulstrode is a big, slow, steady barge. Nothing upsets Bulstrode. He often doesn't even notice when there's a fuss going on around him.

 FUN FACT!
Bulstrode likes to hum lazily to himself. "Dum, de de de dum ..."

He has a very deep, very slo-o-o-w voice

Bulstrode carries lots of life preservers

Sea chase

Thomas asks Bulstrode to help him chase "The Orb of Destiny." It's really a wind-tossed beachball!

🚂 FACT FILE

Role: Carrying cargo to Brendam Docks

Best friend: Skiff

Likes: Doing things at his own pace—slow!

66 Come on, mateys! 99

Rope fender protects his bow

Floating bridge

When Thomas and Kana use Bulstrode as a bridge, he isn't annoyed at all. He's just a bit puzzled.

SKIFF
The little sailboat

This little sailboat has big ideas. Skiff loves to set himself challenges, like sailing in really high winds. He only needs a little help sometimes!

> **"Lighthouse, here I come!"**

 **FACT FILE**

Ambition: To sail to Vicarstown Lighthouse all by himself

Best friend: Bulstrode

Likes: A strong wind

 FUN FACT!
When Skiff gets enough wind in his sail, he can do somersaults.

Skiff in to bat
Skiff is nimble and a good shot. The little sailboat uses his sail to bat a stray beachball back to dry land.

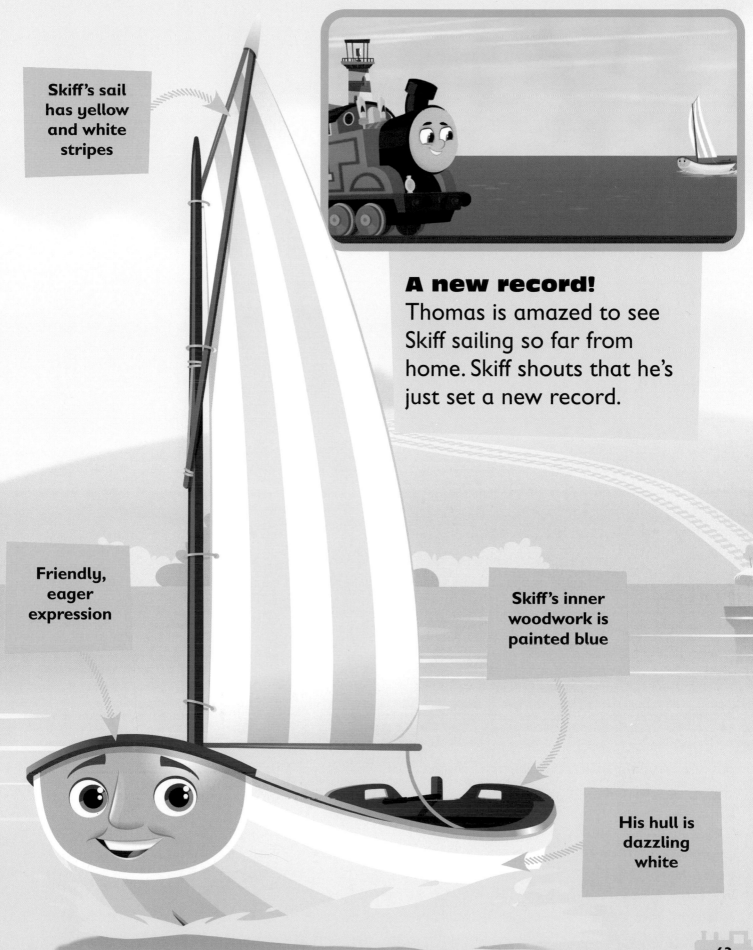

Skiff's sail has yellow and white stripes

A new record!
Thomas is amazed to see Skiff sailing so far from home. Skiff shouts that he's just set a new record.

Friendly, eager expression

Skiff's inner woodwork is painted blue

His hull is dazzling white

LIGHTHOUSE TUNNEL

The tunnel near **Vicarstown** is a favorite with the engines. When they whizz out of the **end**, they get a wonderful view of a jolly **red-and-white lighthouse** against a bright blue sky.

YONG BAO
The tiger train

Yong Bao is from China. This hero engine has made many brave rescues. He teaches Thomas that it's okay to be scared. Even heroes get scared!

Yong Bao has golden stripes

Tiger face design

Yellow lights, like a tiger's eyes

🚂 FACT FILE

Comes from: China

Role: Preventing accidents and saving engines in danger

Likes: Colorful firework displays

A tiger's roar!
The engines meet Yong Bao as he arrives in Sodor. He greets them with a friendly "Roar!"

> 66 **You've got to be scared to be brave.** 99

Facing fears
On a rescue in the mine, Thomas admits he is afraid. Yong Bao says he is scared, too, but he is ready to face his fears to help others.

TROUBLESOME TRUCKS

The worst trucks ever

These bad-mannered cargo trucks are nothing but trouble! They grumble, sneer, and fake injuries to avoid work.

Dirty trick

The green truck sees Nia pulling a new movie screen to a film showing. He flicks dirt at the lovely clean screen, just for fun.

One truck is painted olive green

> **"Hey, my wheel is loose!"**

FUN FACT!
When their schemes go wrong, the trucks blame each other.

It's for real!
From Lookout Mountain, Thomas sees a truck going out of control. This time, it's for real ...

 **FACT FILE**

Roles: Carrying cargo

Likes: Getting the engines in a jumble

Dislikes: Hard work

The other truck is painted reddish-brown

HAROLD
The helpful helicopter

Who needs rails when you have rotors? Harold the helicopter patrols the skies over Sodor, on the lookout for emergencies going on below.

Farm flight
Nia has cows to deliver to McColl's Farm, but she's stuck in a jam. Will Harold give them all a lift? Roger that!

 **FACT FILE**

Likes: Saving the day

Role: Rescuing anyone in trouble and assisting with deliveries

Motto: "Happy to help"

Keep it up!
Harold offers airborne support when Thomas has to get a submarine down Cannonball Curve.

"Roger that ... over and out!"

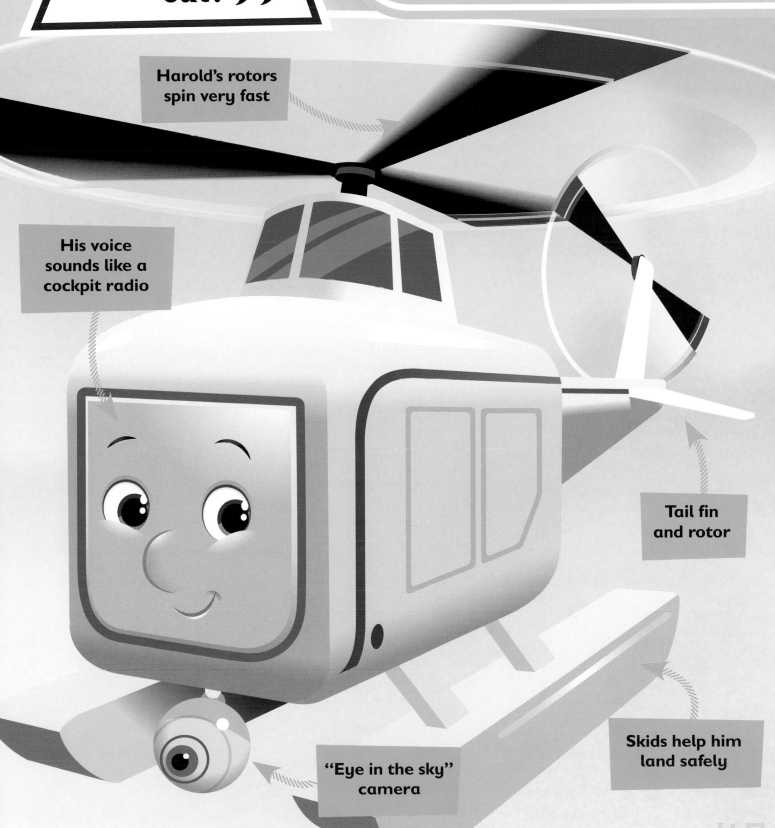

Harold's rotors spin very fast

His voice sounds like a cockpit radio

Tail fin and rotor

"Eye in the sky" camera

Skids help him land safely

KANA
The electric engine

Super-speedy Kana from Japan is the first electric engine to live in Sodor. She loves to race and creates gusts of wind wherever she goes!

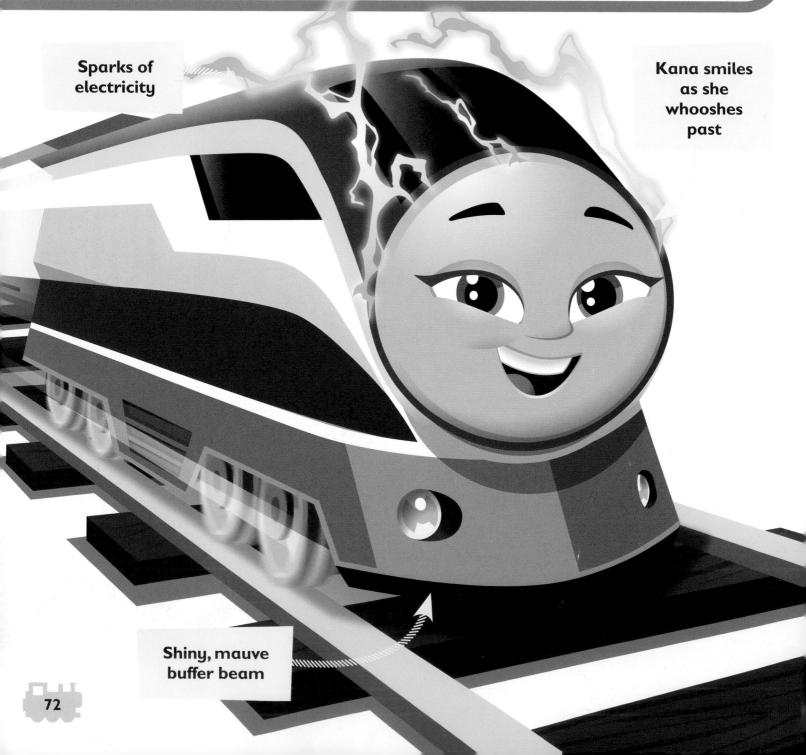

Sparks of electricity

Kana smiles as she whooshes past

Shiny, mauve buffer beam

72

S-l-o-w d-o-w-n
Thomas reminds Kana that if she slows down a little, she'll notice all the lovely flowers and butterflies around her.

66 Electric! Thanks, Thomas! 99

FACT FILE

Role: Transporting people—in a flash!

Works with: All the engines

Likes: Doing everything fast

Just in time!
On the Sodor Cup race course, Kenji stops Kana from hurtling off the rails!

FUN FACT!
Kana has mirror-shiny sides that Thomas loves to makes faces in!

Kana has to stop at a **charging pad** whenever she wants to **power up**. One day, Sandy connected a **wind turbine** to the charging pad. When the **wind** spun the blades, **electricity** flowed and Kana was all charged up—and **ready to go!**

66 **It's not a windmill! It's a wind turbine!** 99

said Kana

Riff AND Jiff
Perfect partners

Riff and Jiff are in the race for the Sodor Cup. These happy high-speed engines just love to compliment each other—and the other entrants, too.

Upbeat duo
Even when the track in front of them breaks, the positive pair keep smiling. Oh well, these things happen!

Riff's lining is bright yellow

> 66 Hi there! You guys are looking good! 99

FUN FACT!

Riff and Jiff like to high-five each other with their front wheels.

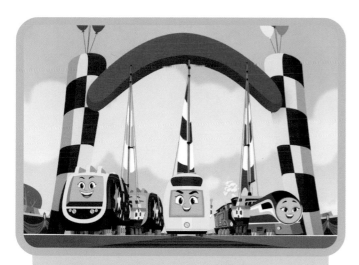

Ready to race

Riff and Jiff are very good-natured. They wish their rivals good luck before the race.

🚂 **FACT FILE**

Home: The mainland

Best friend: Each other. They are totally inseparable.

Likes: A fair, friendly race

Turquoise lining around Jiff's face

Stars are turquoise and yellow

She sports a pink and yellow stars design

CANNONBALL CURVE

It's a wild ride down Cannonball Curve! This **twisty track** spirals around a tall **mountain** to the north of Sodor. Any engine taking the curves too fast could easily **lose control**. Poor **Kana** has learned this lesson the hard way.

FARONA AND FREDERICO

The speedy show-offs

This electric duo visits Sodor to enter the race for the Sodor Cup. They're fast, flashy, and very full of themselves.

66 **We've got the wins to back up our talk!** 99

Sleek yellow and black paintwork

Like Frederico, Farona is an electric engine

Fancy friends

Diesel is eager to befriend the glamorous couple. He changes his tune when he sees them cheating.

🚂 **FACT FILE**

Home: The mainland

Ambition: To win every race they enter

Likes: Cups, trophies, and cheering crowds

Color scheme is reverse of Farona's

No sympathy

When Kana comes off the track at Cannonball Curve, Farona and Frederico just laugh.

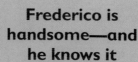

Frederico is handsome—and he knows it

81

HIRO
The wise teacher

All the engines look up to Hiro. He is calm, kind, and wise. When Thomas and Kana enter the Sodor Cup, Hiro proves to be a great trainer, too.

Front lamp gives a golden glow

Hiro has gold boiler bands

Red wheels match his fender

51

Keep calm!

Farona and Frederico taunt Kana, hoping she will make a mistake. Hiro urges her to stay calm.

FACT FILE

Comes from: Japan

Works with: Everyone

Top advice: There's something good in every engine. You just have to find it.

Never give up

When Thomas feels like giving up, Hiro appears in a cloud of steam with words of encouragement.

66 Being calm helps you do anything. 99

FUN FACT!
Thomas keeps a portrait of Hiro in his shed as inspiration.

BRUNO
The brilliant brake car

Bruno travels backward, which suits his unique view of the world. He loves schedules and routine, and really, really, really dislikes surprises.

FUN FACT!
When Bruno gets excited, his lantern spins and flashes.

Did you know?

Bruno is based on an old caboose, which is a type of American brake car.

Number 43 on Bruno's side

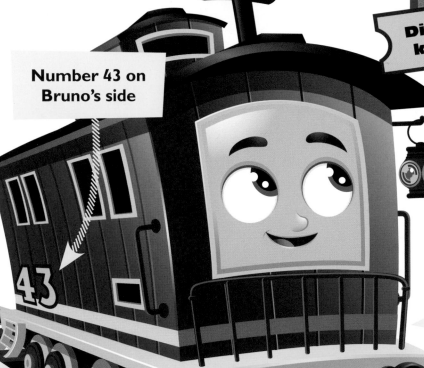

He has a black metal railing at the front

Yellow ladder

WHIFF

The recycler engine

Whiff's job is trash—and he loves it! He works at the Recycling Plant in Sodor, gathering all kinds of waste and sorting it for reuse.

> **66 My name's Whiff because I'm a bit smelly. 99**

 FUN FACT!
Whiff is a bit of a tech whiz who enjoys inventing things.

Whiff wears big, round glasses

He usually has splotches of dirt on him

🚂 **FACT FILE**

Home: Recycling Plant

Role: Processing trash and broken machine parts

Dislikes: Anything going to waste

Bright red buffer beam

LOOKOUT MOUNTAIN

High on Lookout Mountain is an old, abandoned **rail station**. Even higher is a **lookout point** with a breathtaking **view of Sodor**. It's the perfect place for Thomas and his pals to have their **clubhouse**!

GLOSSARY

Barge
A long, flat-bottomed boat used to carry goods.

Boiler
The part of a steam engine where water is heated to make steam.

Brake car
A wagon at the end of a train that contains a brake.

Buffer
A device that reduces the impact when rail vehicles come together.

Coupling hook
A curved hook used to connect rail vehicles together.

Diesel engine
A train that is powered by diesel fuel.

Fender
A frame or bumper that reduces damage from collisions.

Rotors
Long, spinning blades on the top of a helicopter that lift it off the ground.

Shunter
A vehicle used for moving trucks or wagons.

Speeder
A small rail vehicle often used by rail workers to get around.

Steam engine
A train or other vehicle that is powered by steam from boiling water.

Tank engine
A steam engine that carries its fuel and water in tanks alongside the boiler.

Tender engine
A steam engine that carries its fuel and water in a tender car.

INDEX

Senior Editor Selina Wood
Senior Designer Lauren Adams
Designer Thelma-Jane Robb
Production Editor Marc Staples
Senior Production Controller Lloyd Robertson
Proofreader Kayla Dugger
Managing Art Editor Jo Connor
Publishing Director Mark Searle

DK would like to thank Rowenna Otazu
at Mattel for assistance.

First American Edition, 2022
Published in the United States by DK Publishing
1745 Broadway, 20th Floor, New York, NY 10019

Page design copyright © 2022 Dorling Kindersley Limited
DK, a Division of Penguin Random House LLC
22 23 24 25 26 10 9 8 7 6 5 4 3 2 1
001–326955–Nov/2022

THE BRITT ALLCROFT COMPANY

Based on the Railway Series by The Reverend W Awdry.
© 2022 Gullane (Thomas) Limited.
Thomas the Tank Engine & Friends™ and Thomas & Friends™
are trademarks of Gullane (Thomas) Limited.
© 2022 HIT Entertainment Limited. HIT and the HIT logo are
trademarks of HIT Entertainment Limited.

A catalog record for this book
is available from the Library of Congress.
ISBN 978-0-7440-5465-1

Printed and bound in China

For the curious
www.dk.com

**The publisher would like to thank the following for
their kind permission to reproduce their photographs:**

12 Getty Images: Science & Society Picture Library (clb).
33 Dorling Kindersley: Didcot Railway Centre (tl).
51 Alamy Stock Photo: BJ Warnick / Newscom (tr).
84 Alamy Stock Photo: Bruce Leighty (cra).

All other images © 2022 Gullane (Thomas) Limited.

MIX
Paper | Supporting
responsible forestry
FSC™ C018179

This book is made from
Forest Stewardship Council™
certified paper—one small
step in DK's commitment
to a sustainable future.